FOR ORGANS, PIANOS & ELECTRONIC KEYBOARDS

E-Z PLAY TODAY

221

2nd Edition

Carly Simon
Greatest Hits

Cover photo by Heidi Wild

ISBN 978-0-7935-0875-4

HAL•LEONARD®
CORPORATION

7777 W. BLUEMOUND RD. P.O. BOX 13819 MILWAUKEE, WI 53213

E-Z Play® Today Music Notation
© 1975 by HAL LEONARD CORPORATION

E-Z PLAY and EASY ELECTRONIC KEYBOARD MUSIC are registered trademarks of HAL LEONARD CORPORATION.

Visit Hal Leonard Online at
www.halleonard.com

All I Want Is You

Registration 1
Rhythm: Rock or 8 Beat

Words and Music by Carly Simon,
Jacob Brackman and Andy Goldmark

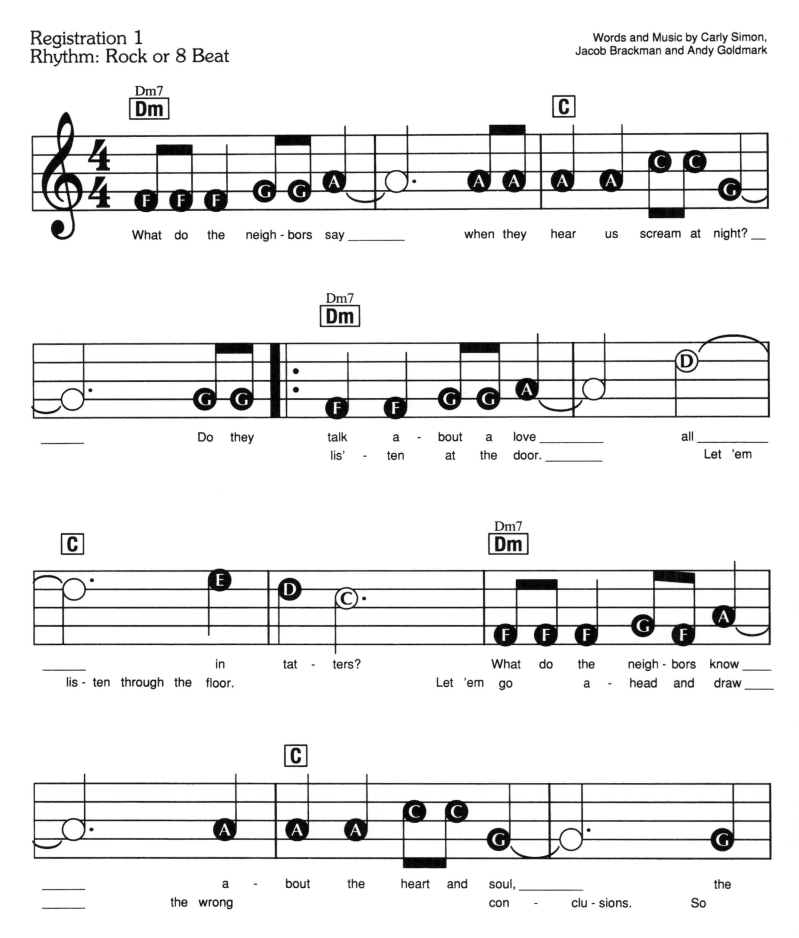

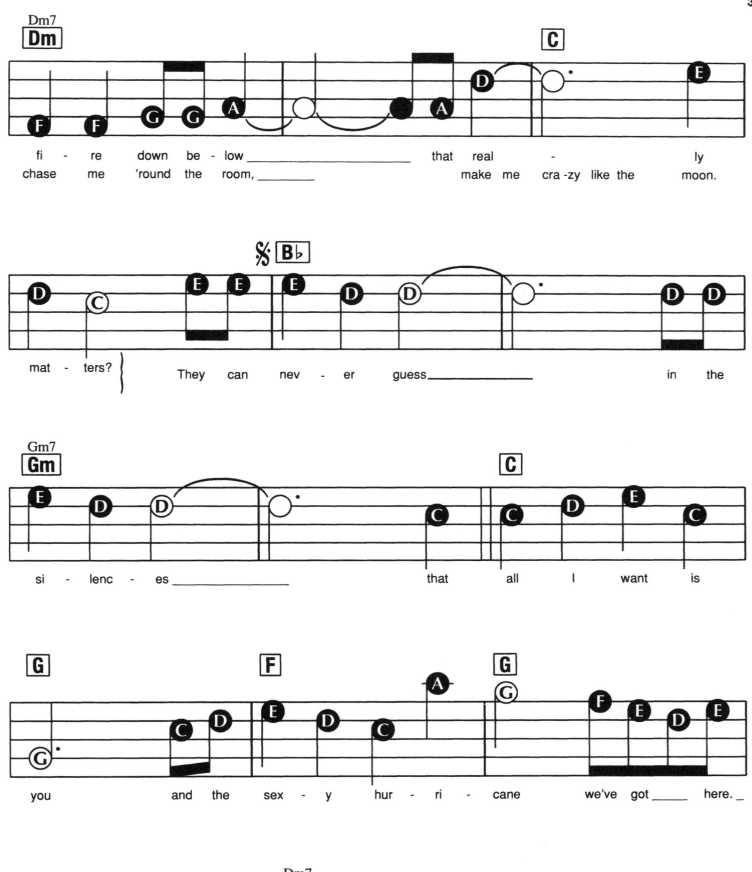

fi - re down be - low _____ that real - ly

chase me 'round the room, _____ make me cra -zy like the moon.

mat - ters? They can nev - er guess_____ in the

si - lenc - es _____ that all I want is

you and the sex - y hur - ri - cane we've got _____ here. _

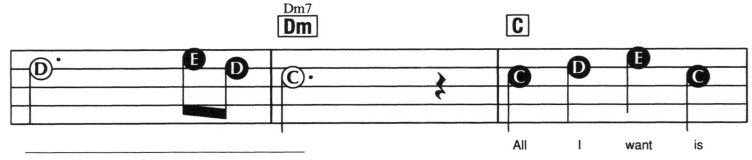

_____ All I want is

4

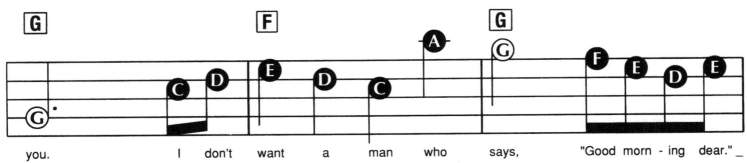

you.   I don't want a man who says,   "Good morn - ing dear." _

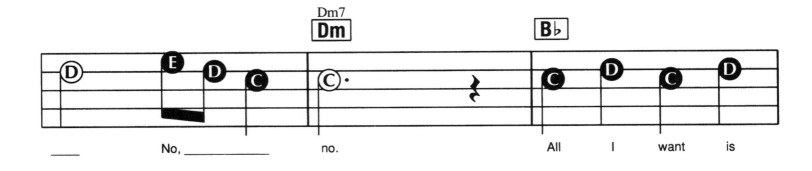

___   No, _____ no.   All   I   want   is

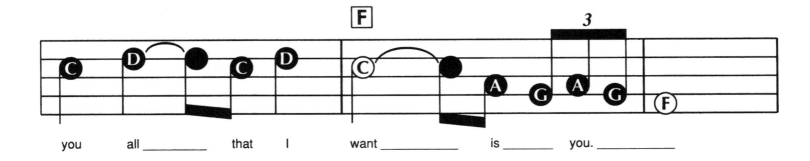

you   all _____ that   I   want _____ is _____ you. _____

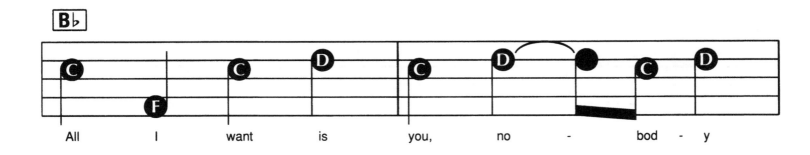

All   I   want   is   you,   no -   bod - y

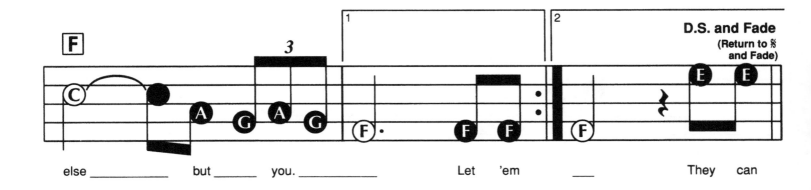

else _____ but _____ you. _____   Let 'em ___ They can

Attitude Dancing

Registration 3
Rhythm: Rock or 8 Beat

Words and Music by Carly Simon
and Jacob Brackman

6

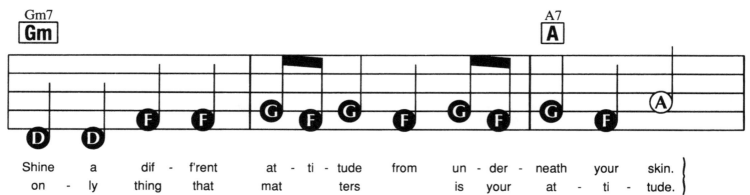

Shine a dif - f'rent at - ti - tude from un - der - neath your skin.
on - ly thing that mat - ters is your at - ti - tude.

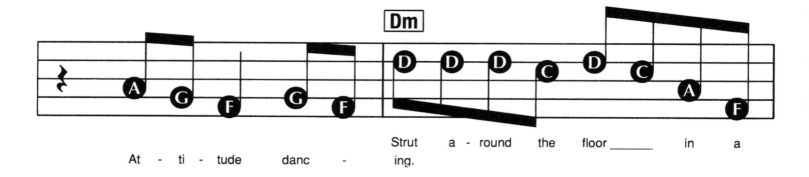

At - ti - tude danc - ing.
Strut a - round the floor _____ in a

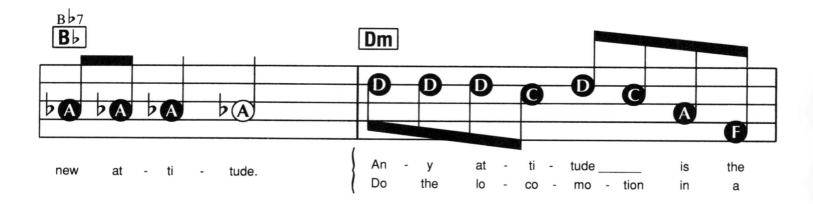

new at - ti - tude.
An - y at - ti - tude _____ is the
Do the lo - co - mo - tion in a

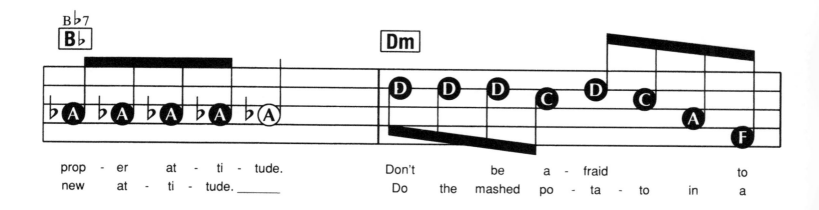

prop - er at - ti - tude.
new at - ti - tude. _____
Don't be a - fraid to
Do the mashed po - ta - to in a

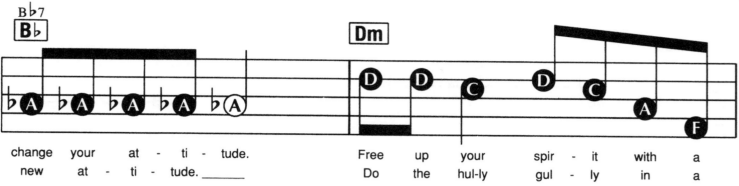

change your at - ti - tude.   Free up your spir - it with a
new at - ti - tude. _____   Do the hul-ly gul - ly in a

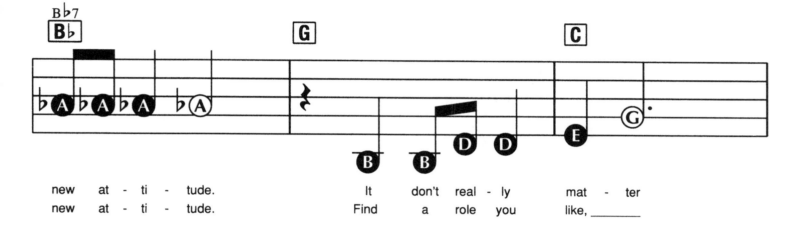

new at - ti - tude.   It don't real - ly mat - ter
new at - ti - tude.   Find a role you like, _____

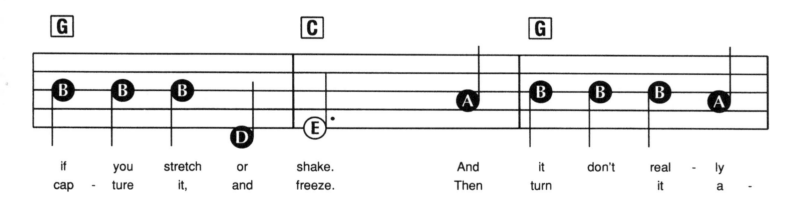

if you stretch or shake.   And it don't real - ly
cap - ture it, or and freeze.   Then turn it a -

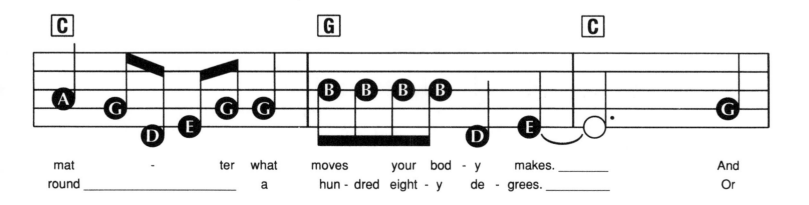

mat - ter what moves your bod - y makes. _____   And
round _____ a hun - dred eight - y de - grees. _____   Or

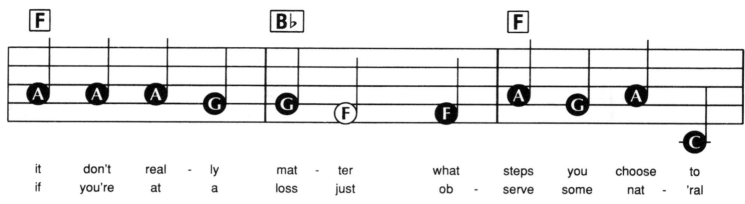

it   don't   real - ly   mat - ter   what   steps   you   choose   to
if   you're   at   a   loss   just   ob - serve   some   nat - 'ral

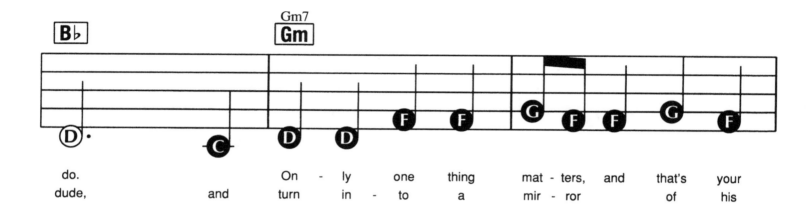

do.   On - ly   one   thing   mat - ters,   and   that's   your
dude,   and   turn   in - to   a   mir - ror   of   his

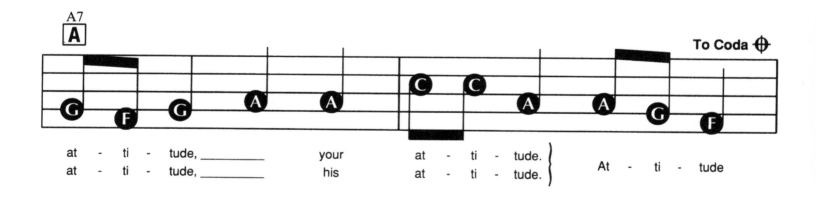

at - ti - tude, _____ your   at - ti - tude.   At - ti - tude
at - ti - tude, _____ his   at - ti - tude.

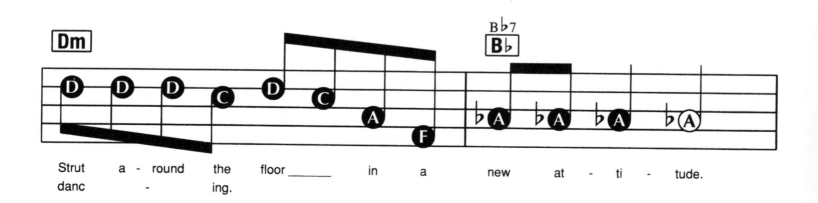

Strut   a - round   the   floor_____   in   a   new   at - ti - tude.
danc - ing.

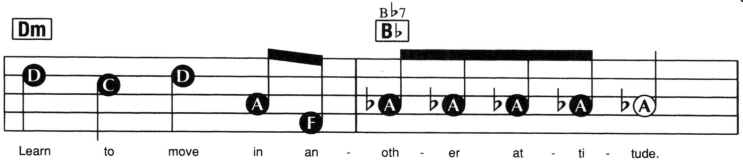

Learn to move in an - oth - er at - ti - tude.

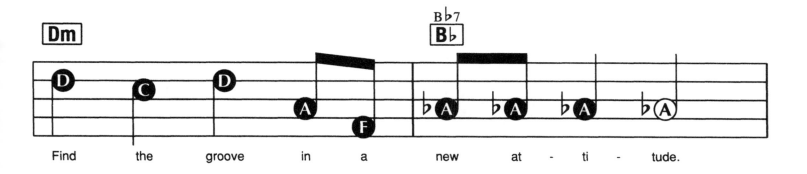

Find the groove in a new at - ti - tude.

D.C. al Coda
(Return to beginning
Play to ⊕
Skip to Coda)

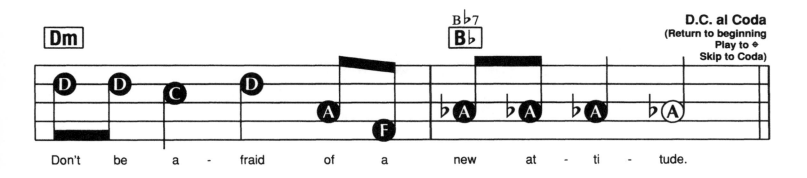

Don't be a - fraid of a new at - ti - tude.

CODA
Repeat and Fade

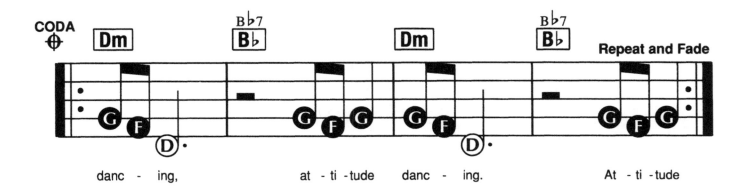

danc - ing, at - ti - tude danc - ing. At - ti - tude

Anticipation

Registration 4
Rhythm: Rock or Jazz Rock

Words and Music by
Carly Simon

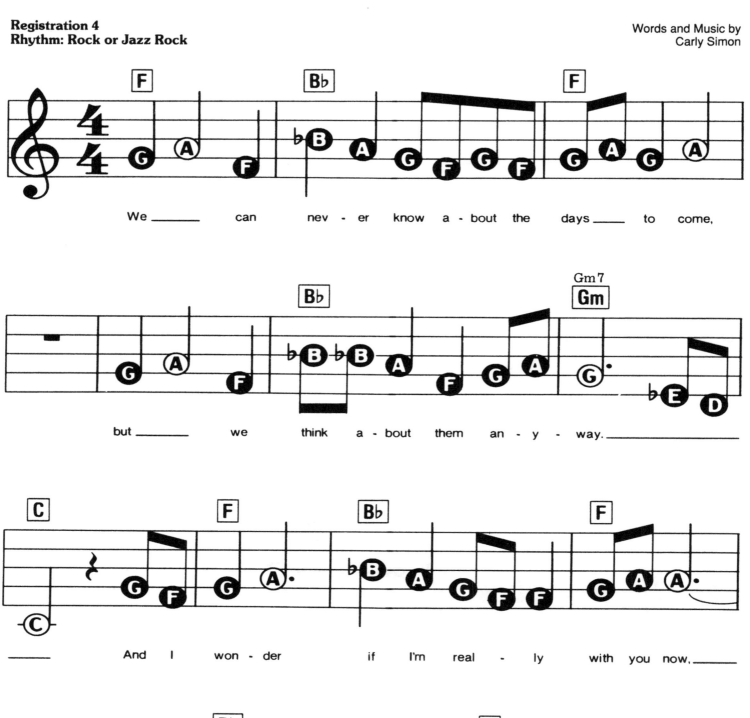

We ___ can nev - er know a - bout the days ___ to come,

but ___ we think a - bout them an - y - way. ___

And I won - der if I'm real - ly with you now, ___

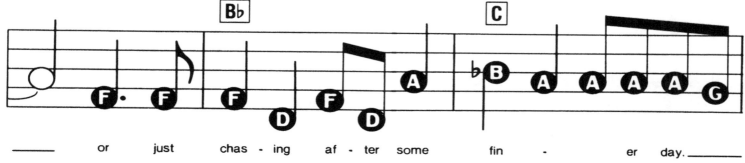

___ or just chas - ing af - ter some fin - er day. ___

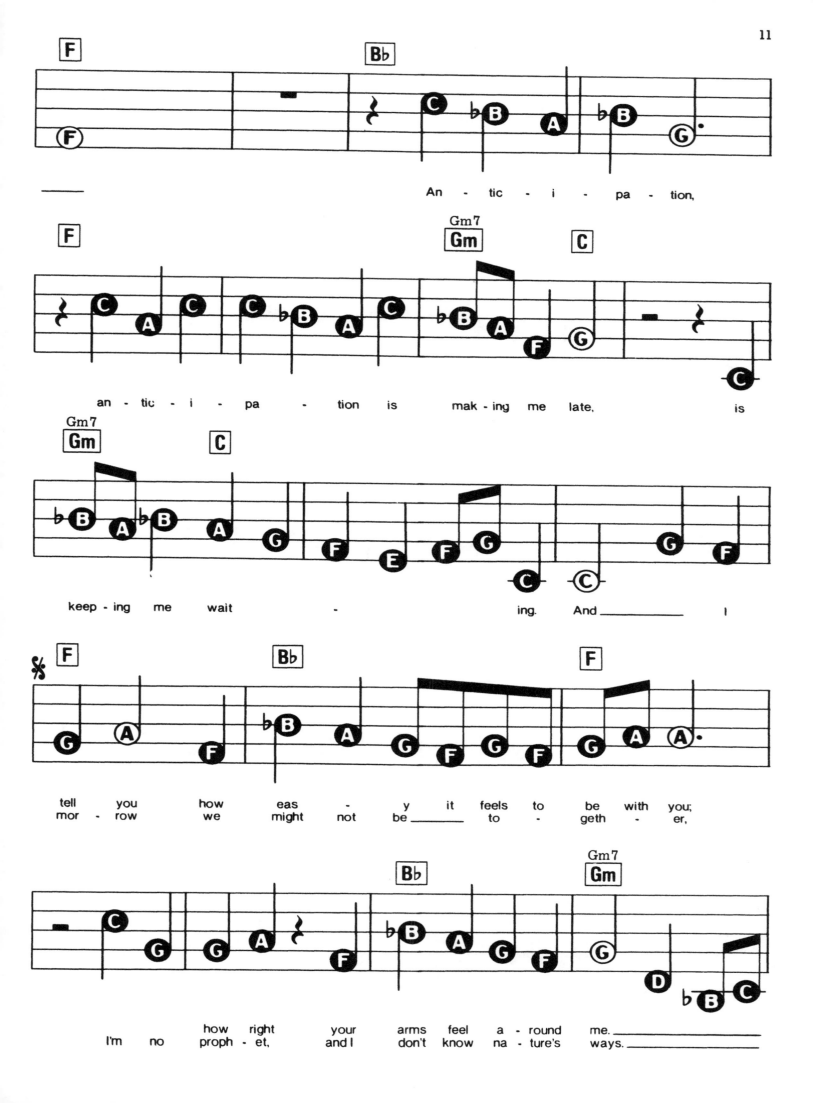

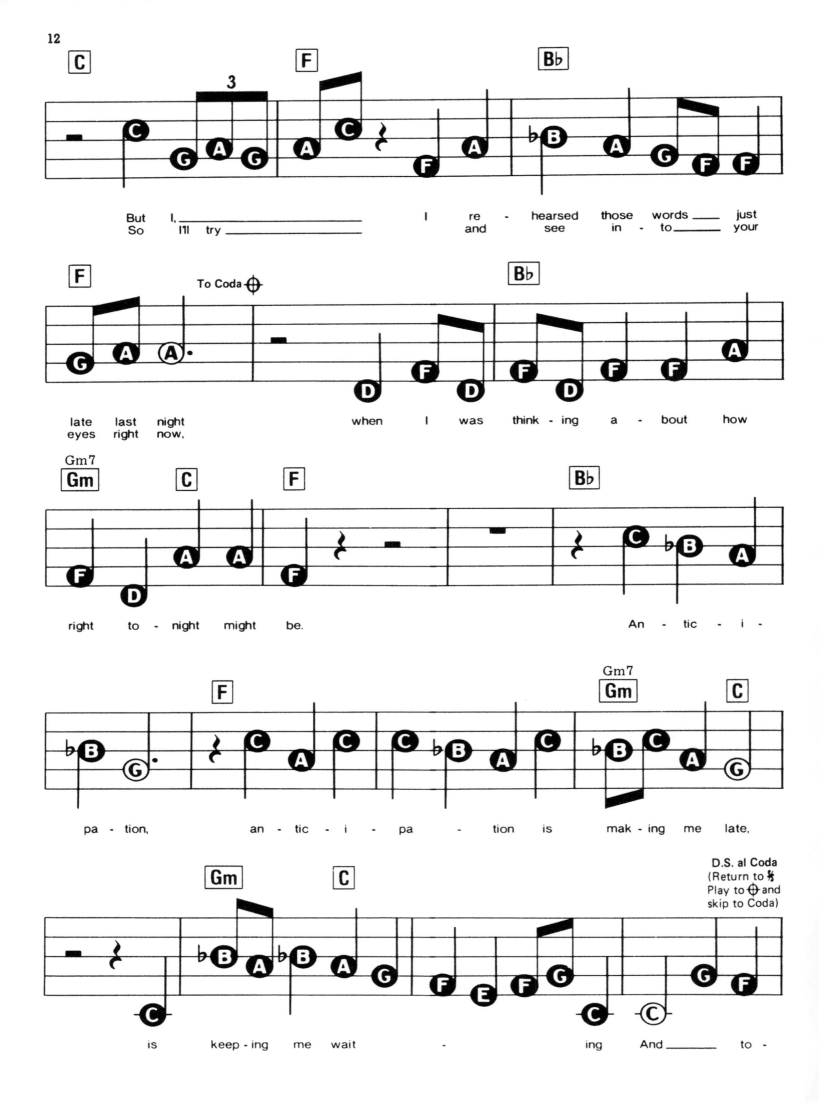

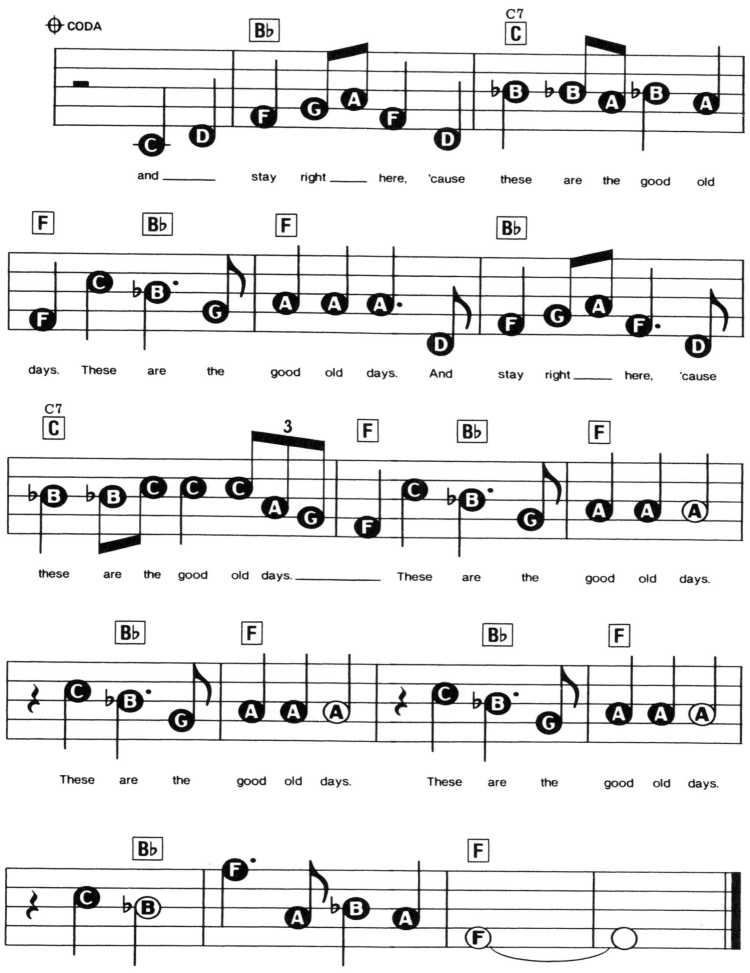

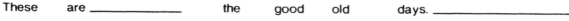

Coming Around Again
from the Paramount Picture HEARTBURN

Registration 9
Rhythm: Slow Rock or 12 Beat

Words and Music by
Carly Simon

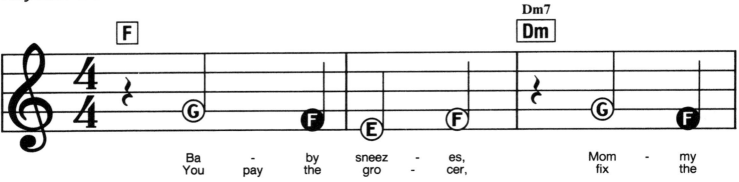

Ba - by sneez - es, Mom - my
You pay the gro - cer, fix my

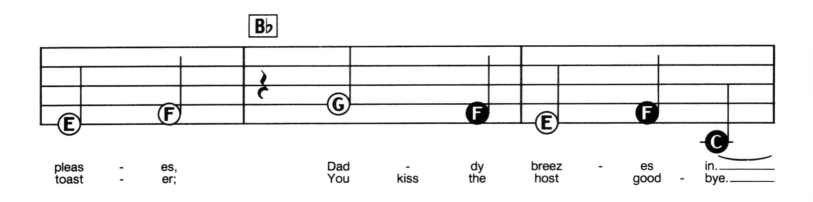

pleas - es, Dad - dy breez - es in.
toast - er; You kiss the host good - bye.

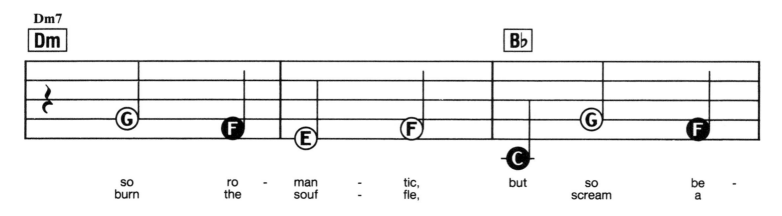

So you good on pa - per,
Then you break a win - dow,

so ro - man - tic, but so be -
burn the man souf - fle, scream a

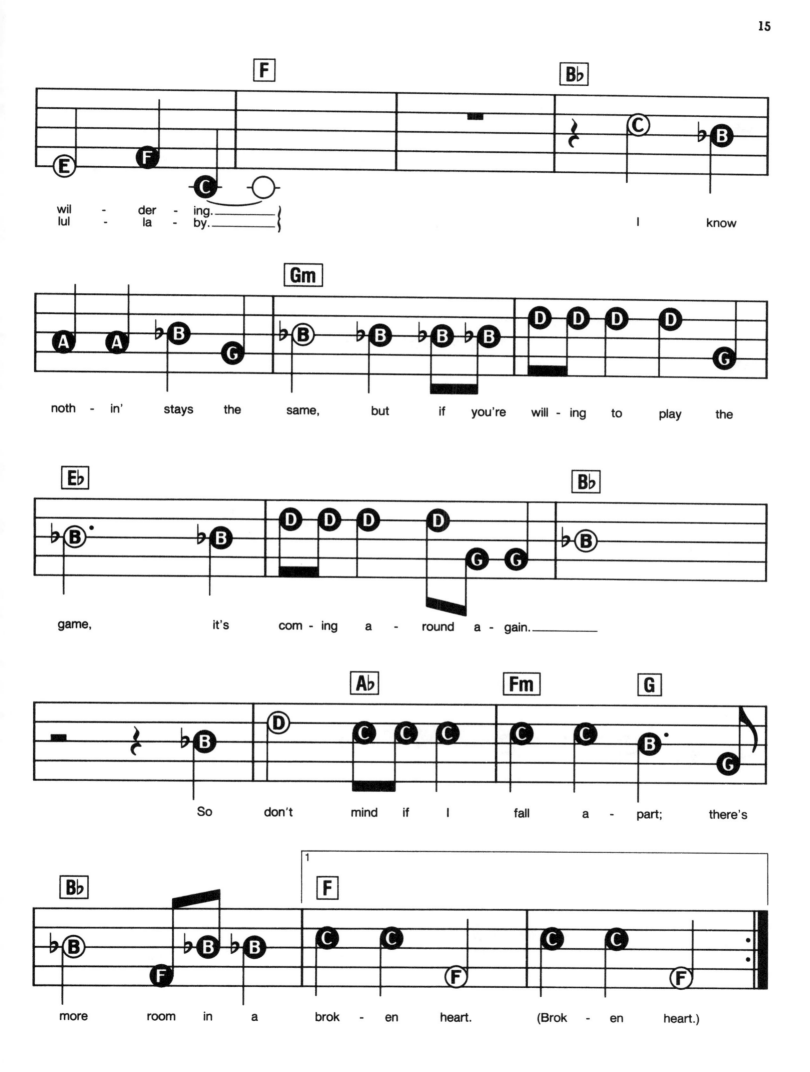

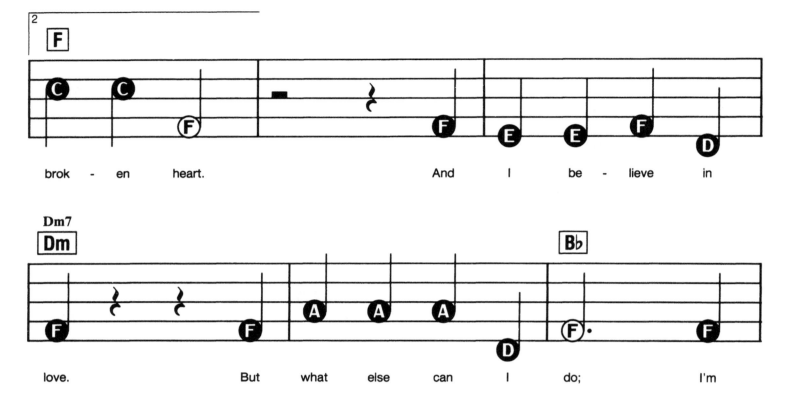

brok - en heart.   And   I   be - lieve in

love.   But   what   else   can   I   do;   I'm

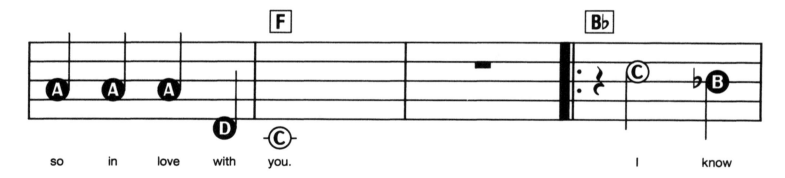

so   in   love   with   you.   I   know

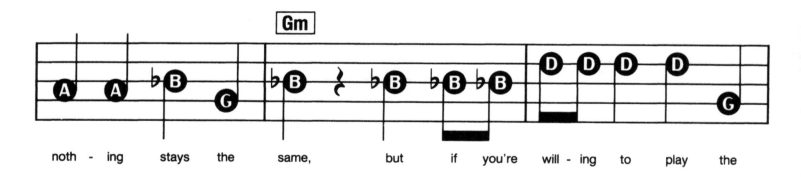

noth - ing   stays   the   same,   but   if   you're   will - ing   to   play   the

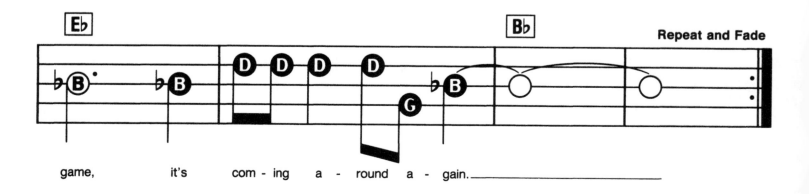

game,   it's   com - ing   a - round   a - gain.

Haven't Got Time for the Pain

Registration 9
Rhythm: Rock or Disco

Words and Music by Carly Simon
and Jacob Brackman

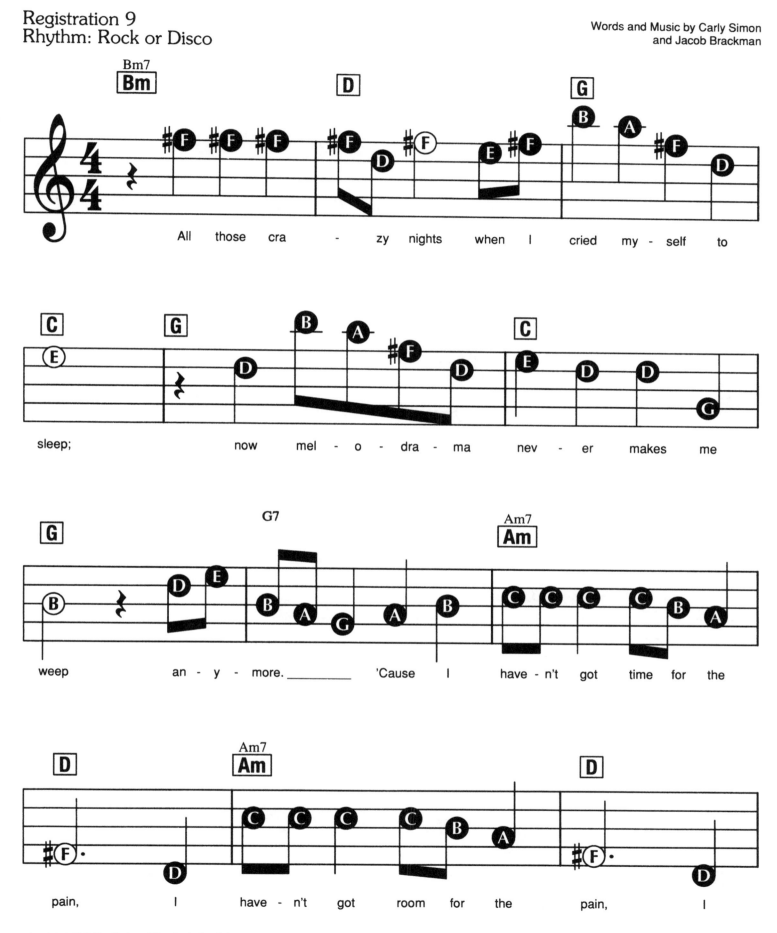

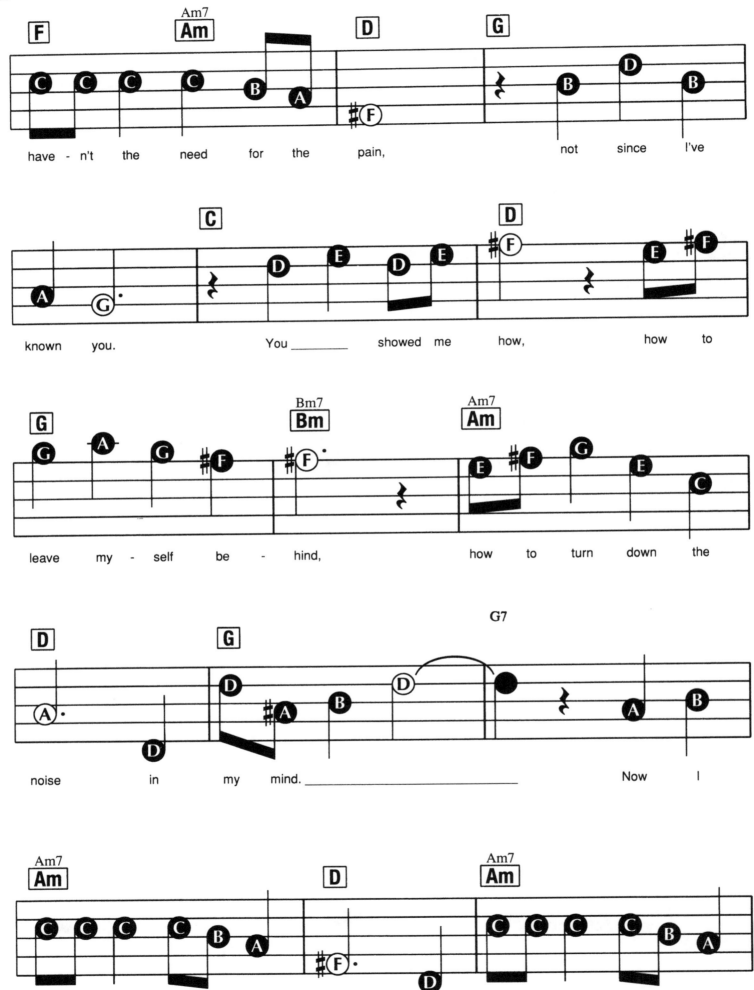

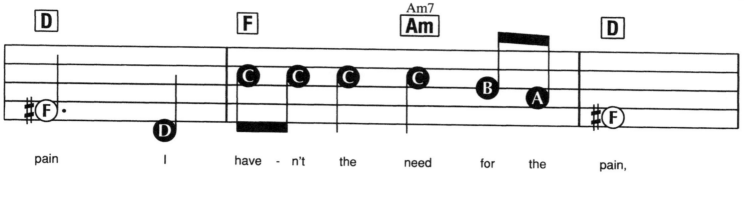

pain   I   have - n't   the   need   for   the   pain,

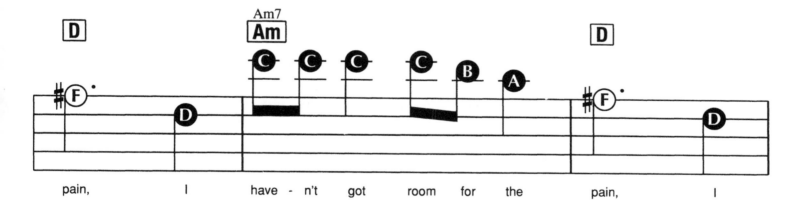

not   since   I've   known   you.   I   have - n't   got   time   for   the

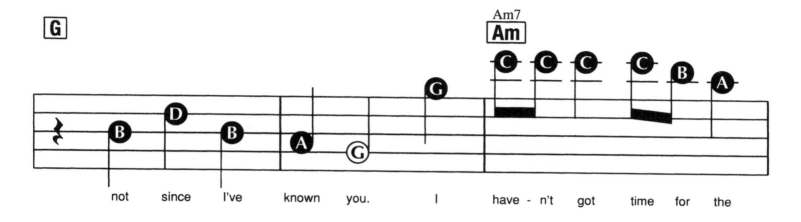

pain,   I   have - n't   got   room   for   the   pain,   I

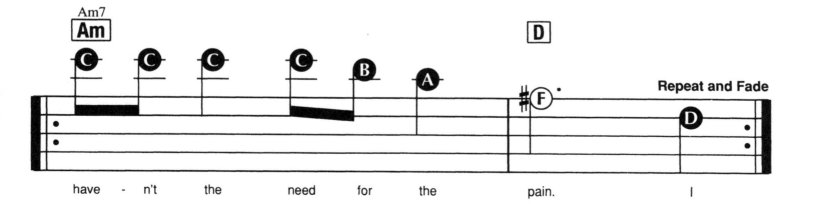

have - n't   the   need   for   the   pain.   I

Jesse

Registration 5
Rhythm: Pop or Rock

Words and Music by Carly Simon
and Mike Mainieri

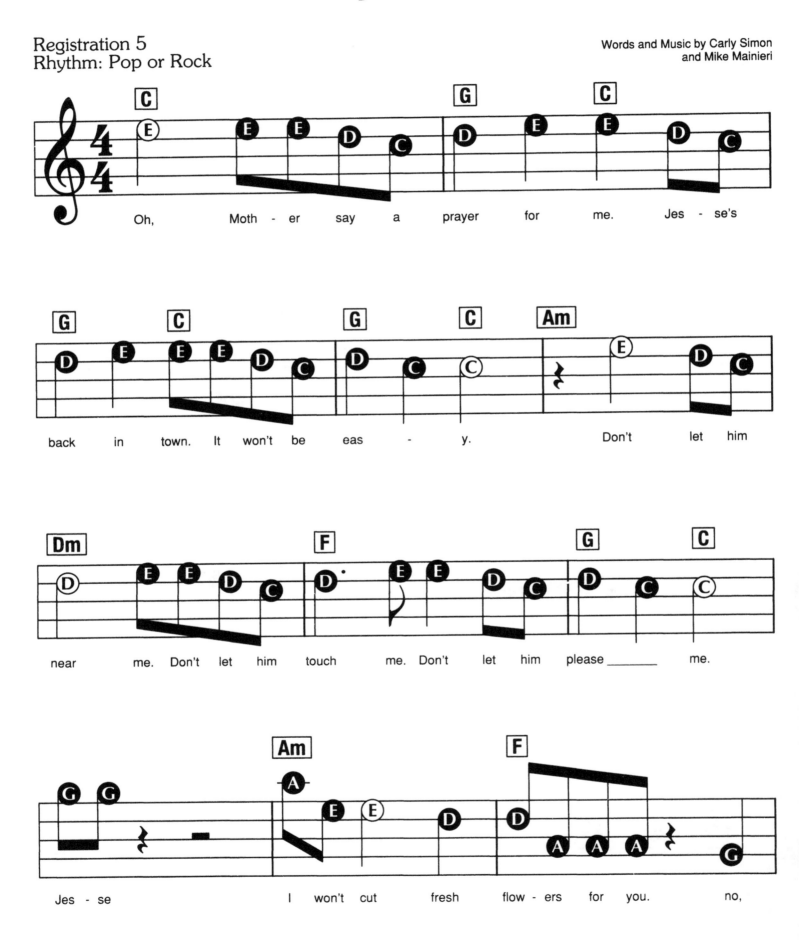

Oh, Moth - er say a prayer for me. Jes - se's

back in town. It won't be eas - y. Don't let him

near me. Don't let him touch me. Don't let him please _____ me.

Jes - se I won't cut fresh flow - ers for you. no,

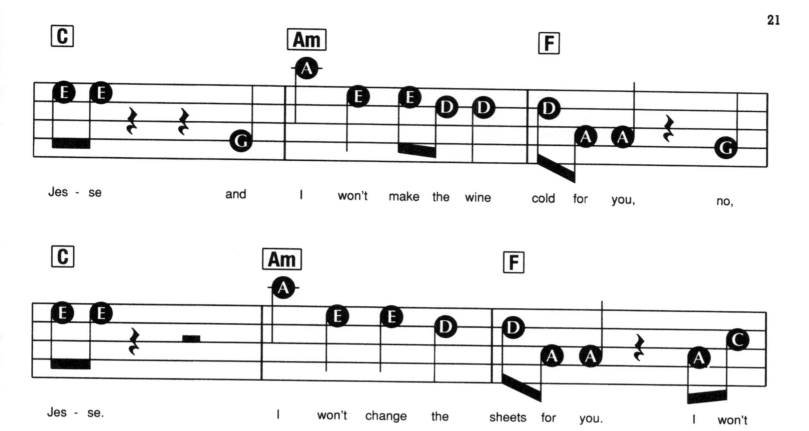

Jes - se and I won't make the wine cold for you, no,

Jes - se. I won't change the sheets for you. I won't

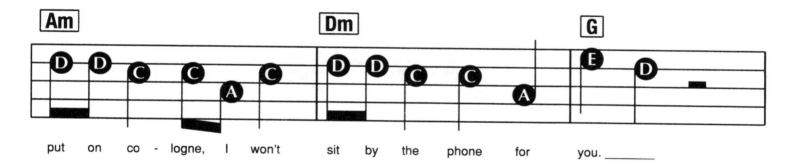

put on co - logne, I won't sit by the phone for you. _____

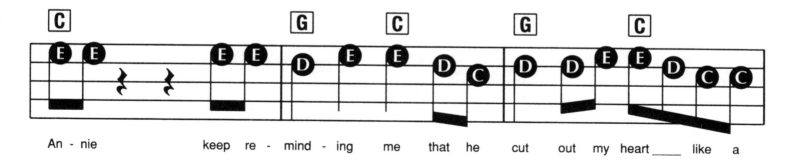

An - nie keep re - mind - ing me that he cut out my heart ____ like a

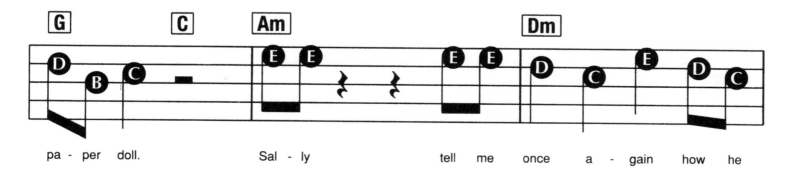

pa - per doll. Sal - ly tell me once a - gain how he

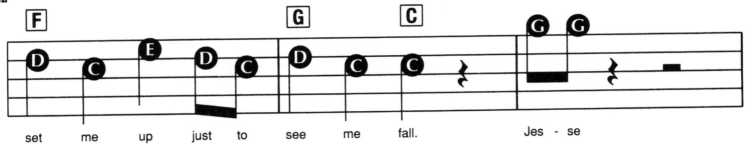

set me up just to see me fall. Jes - se

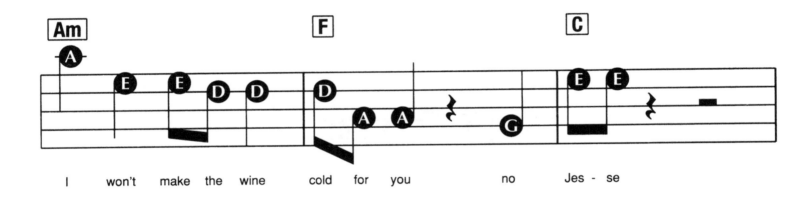

I won't cut fresh flow - ers for you, no, Jes - se and

I won't make the wine cold for you no Jes - se

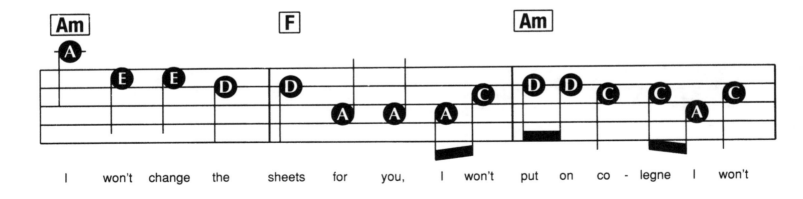

I won't change the sheets for you, I won't put on co - legne I won't

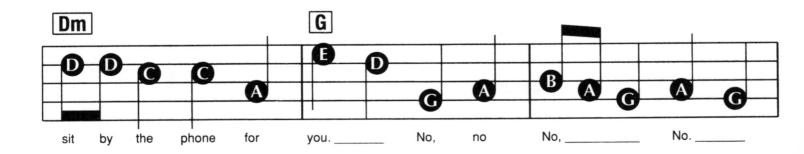

sit by the phone for you. _____ No, no No, _____ No. _____

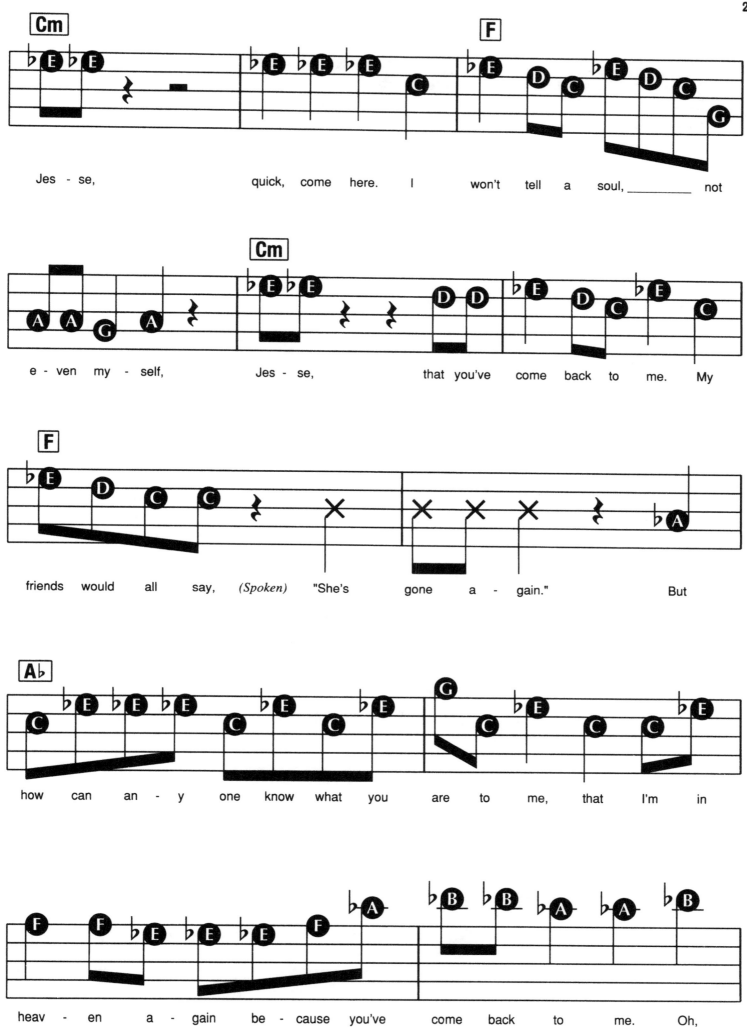

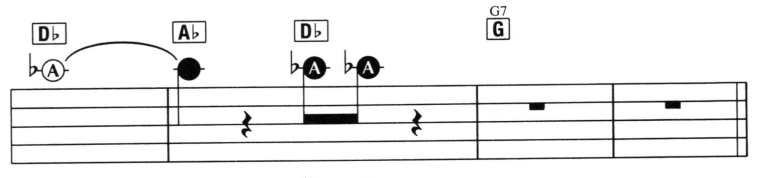

Jes - se

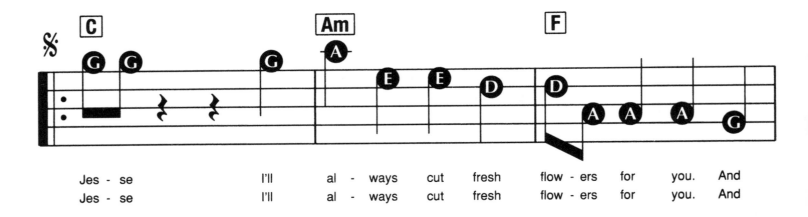

Jes - se   I'll   al - ways   cut   fresh   flow - ers   for   you.   And
Jes - se   I'll   al - ways   cut   fresh   flow - ers   for   you.   And

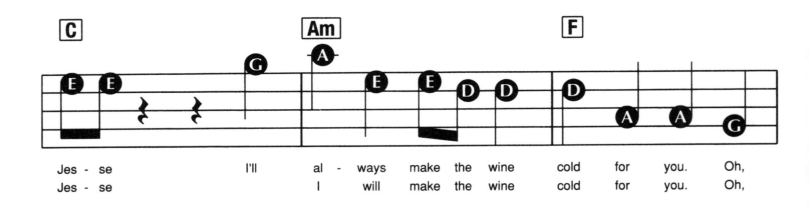

Jes - se   I'll   al - ways   make   the   wine   cold   for   you.   Oh,
Jes - se   I   will   make   the   wine   cold   for   you.   Oh,

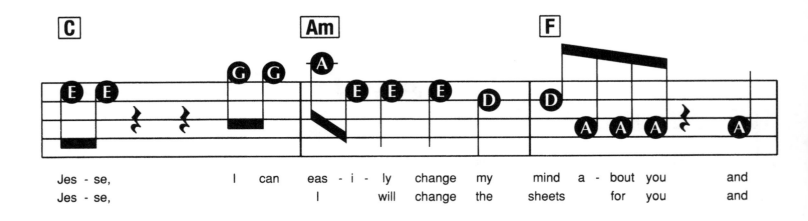

Jes - se,   I   can   eas - i - ly   change   my   mind   a - bout   you   and
Jes - se,   I   will   change   the   sheets   for   you   and

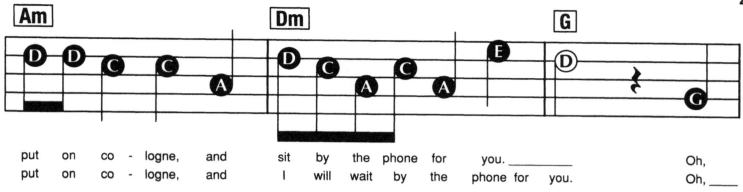

put on co - logne, and sit by the phone for you. _____ Oh,
put on co - logne, and I will wait by the phone for you. Oh, ____

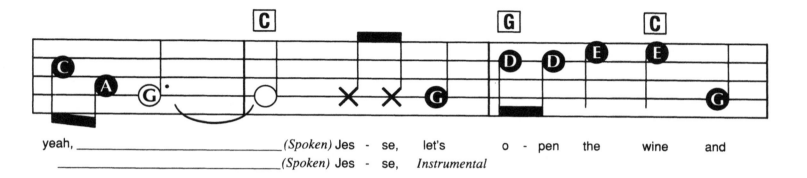

yeah, _____ (Spoken) Jes - se, let's o - pen the wine and
_____ (Spoken) Jes - se, *Instrumental*

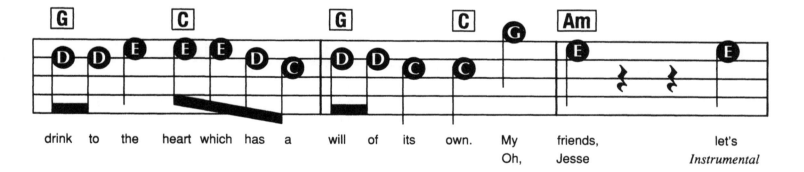

drink to the heart which has a will of its own. My friends, let's
Oh, Jesse *Instrumental*

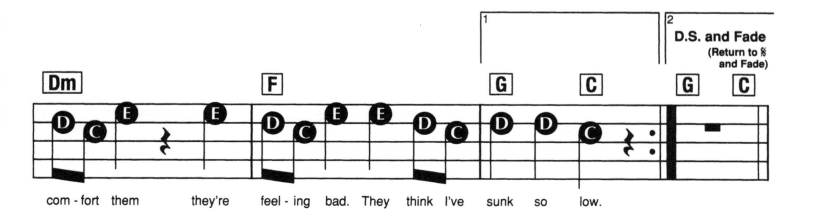

com - fort them they're feel - ing bad. They think I've sunk so low.

Let the River Run
Theme from the Motion Picture WORKING GIRL

Registration 3
Rhythm: Rock or 8 Beat

Words and Music by
Carly Simon

Let the riv - er run, let all the dream - ers wake the
Sil - ver cit - ies rise; let the morn - ing lights the streets that

na - tion. Come, _____ the new Je - ru - sa -
lead them. And si - rens call them

lem. _____
on with a

song. _____
It's ask - ing for the

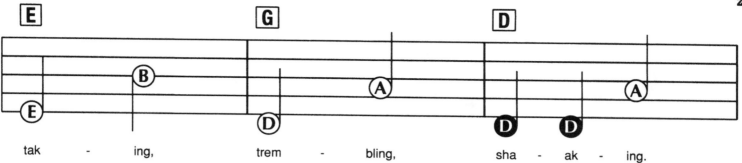

tak - ing, trem - bling, sha - ak - ing.

Oh, _____ my heart is ach - ing. We're

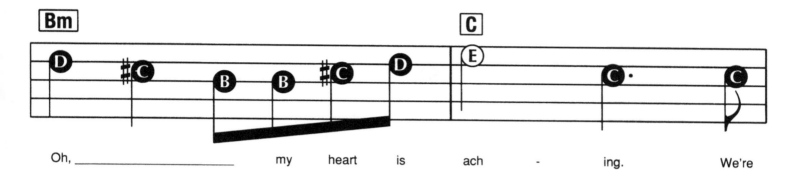

com - ing to the edge, run - ning on the wa - ter,

A7

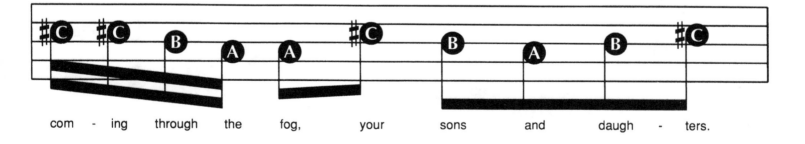

com - ing through the fog, your sons and daugh - ters.

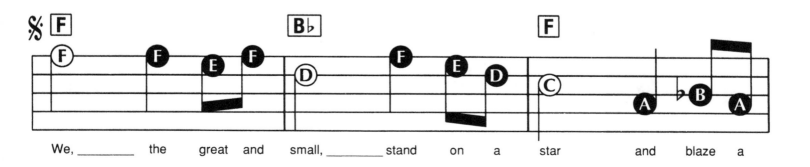

We, _____ the great and small, _____ stand on a star and blaze a

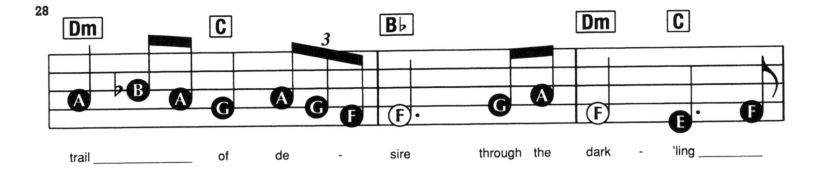

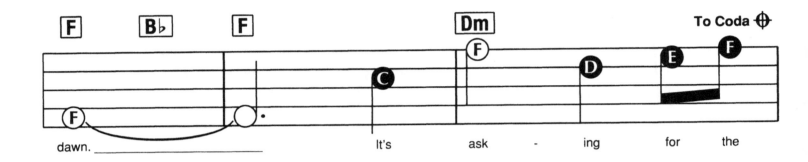

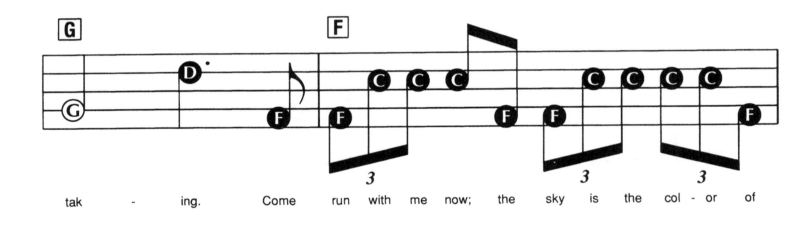

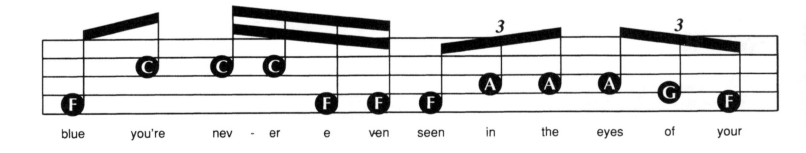

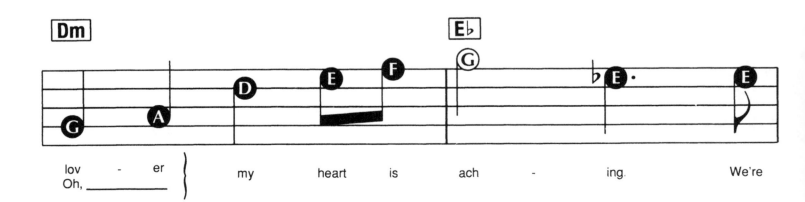

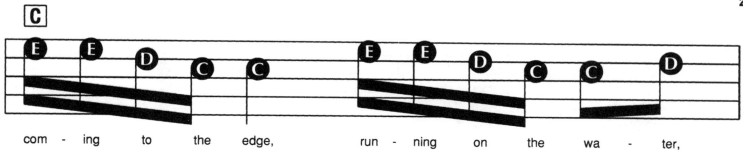

com - ing to the edge, run - ning on the wa - ter,

C7

D.S. al Coda
(Return to %
Play to ⊕
Skip to Coda)

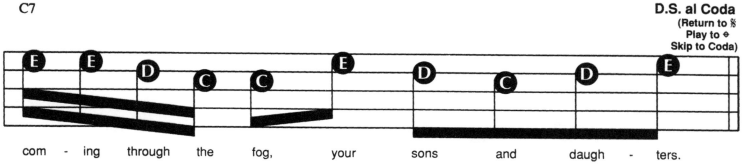

com - ing through the fog, your sons and daugh - ters.

CODA
⊕

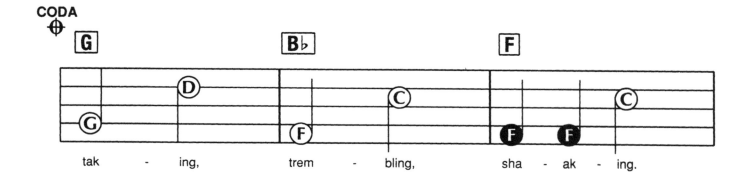

tak - ing, trem - bling, sha - ak - ing.

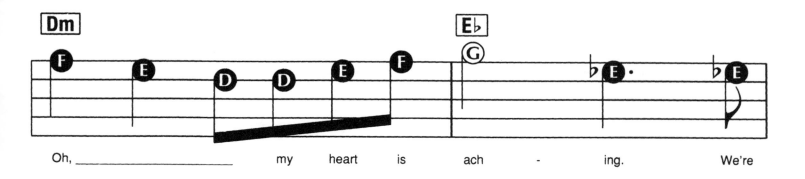

Oh, _____ my heart is ach - ing. We're

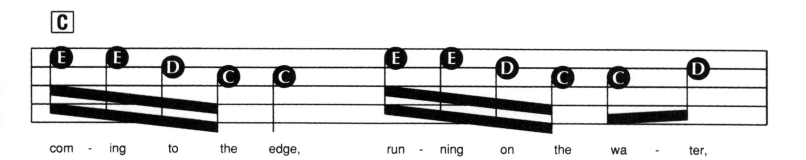

com - ing to the edge, run - ning on the wa - ter,

C7

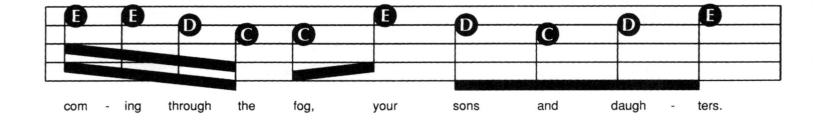

com - ing through the fog, your sons and daugh - ters.

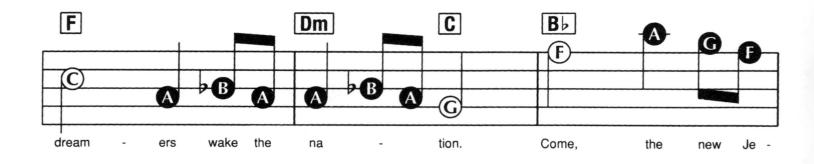

Let _____ the riv - er run. _____ Let all the

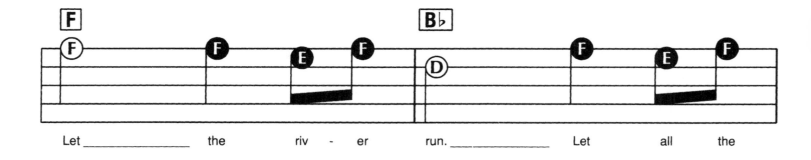

dream - ers wake the na - tion. Come, the new Je -

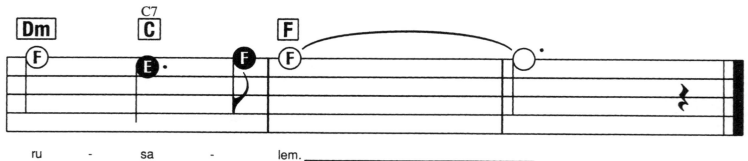

ru - sa - lem. _____

Mockingbird

Registration 4
Rhythm: Rock or 8 Beat

Words and Music by Inez Foxx and Charlie Foxx
Additional Lyrics by James Taylor

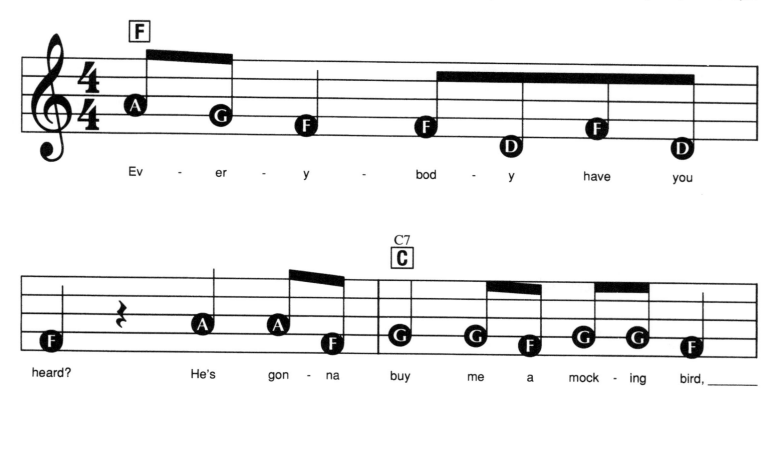

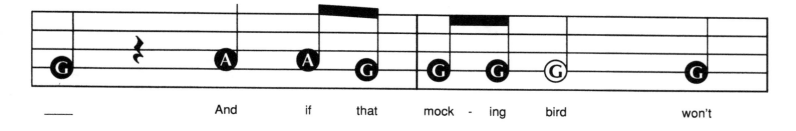

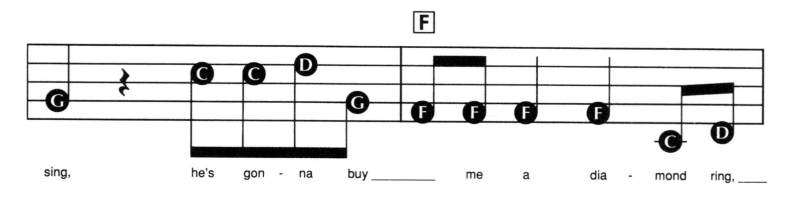

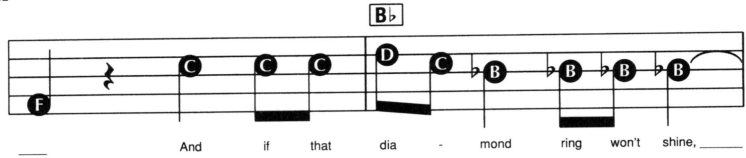

And if that dia - mond ring won't shine, _____

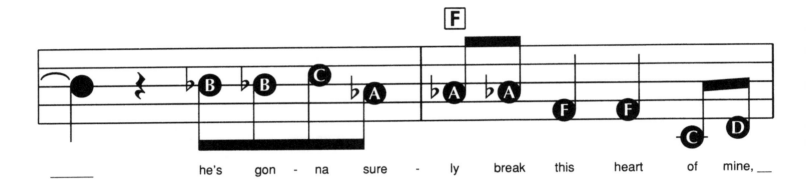

_____ he's gon - na sure - ly break this heart of mine, ___

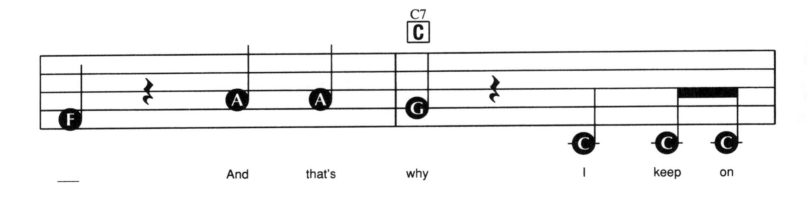

___ And that's why I keep on

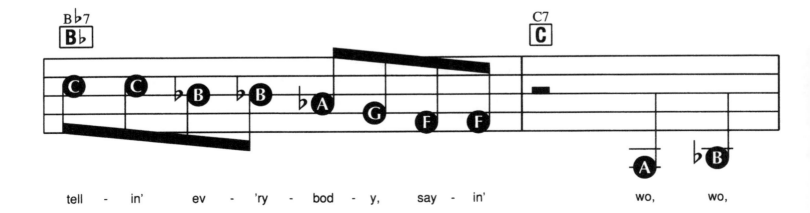

tell - in' ev - 'ry - bod - y, say - in' wo, wo,

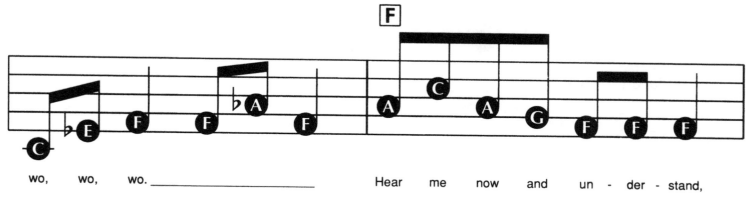

wo, wo, wo. _____ Hear me now and un - der - stand,

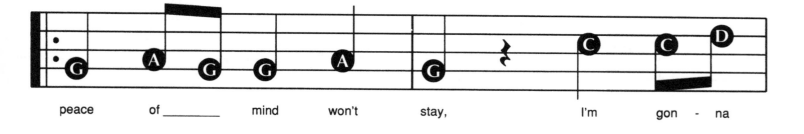

he's gon - na find me some peace of mind. And if that

peace of _____ mind won't stay, I'm gon - na

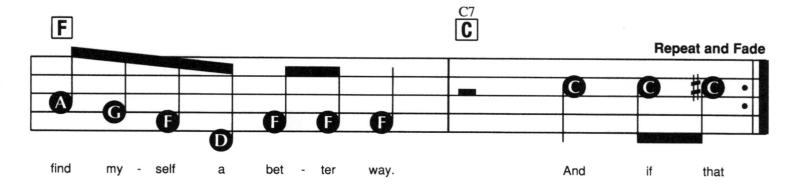

find my - self a bet - ter way. And if that

Nobody Does It Better
from THE SPY WHO LOVED ME

Registration 4
Rhythm: Ballad or Rock

Lyrics by Carole Bayer Sager
Music by Marvin Hamlisch

1,3 No - bod - y does it bet - ter
2 No - bod - y does it bet - ter

makes me feel sad for the rest.
some - times I wish some - one could.

No - bod - y does it
No - bod - y does it

half as good as you.
quite the way you do.

Did

Ba - by, you're the best.
you have to be so good?

The

I was - n't look - in'
way that you hold me

but
when

some - how you found me.
ev - er you hold me.

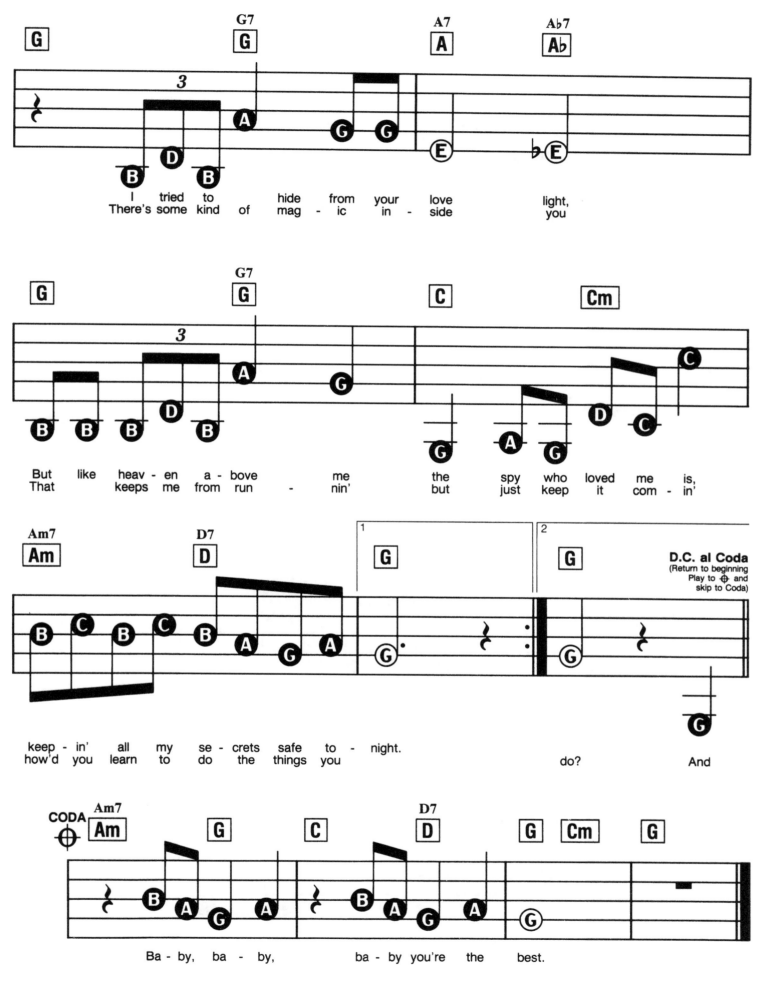

The Right Thing to Do

Registration 2
Rhythm: Rock or 8 Beat

Words and Music by
Carly Simon

1. There's noth-in' you can do to turn me a-way,

2,3 *(See additional lyrics)*

noth - in' an - y - one can say. You're with me now, and as

long as you stay, lov - in' you's the right thing to do.

Lov - in' you's the right thing. Oh,_____ I

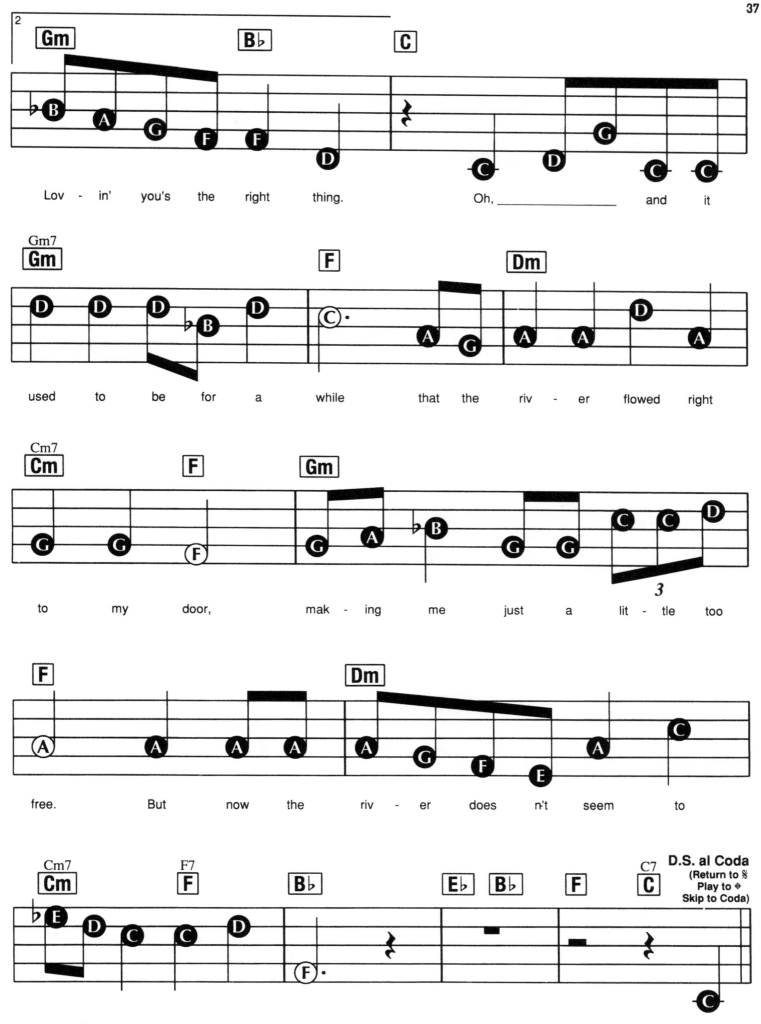

Lov - in' you's the right thing. Oh, _____ and it

used to be for a while that the riv - er flowed right

to my door, mak - ing me just a lit - tle too

free. But now the riv - er does - n't seem to

stop here ____ an - y - more. 3. You

D.S. al Coda
(Return to %
Play to ✛
Skip to Coda)

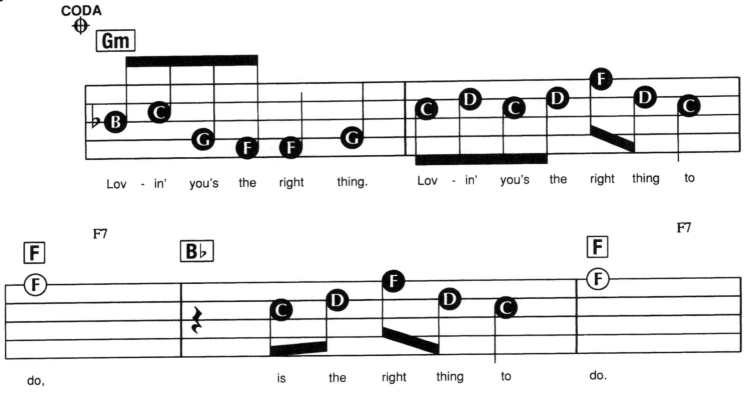

Lov - in' you's the right thing. Lov - in' you's the right thing to

do, is the right thing to do.

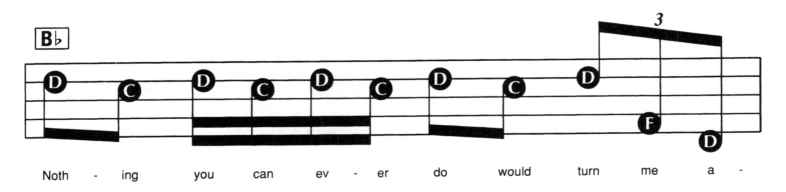

Noth - ing you can ev - er do would turn me a -

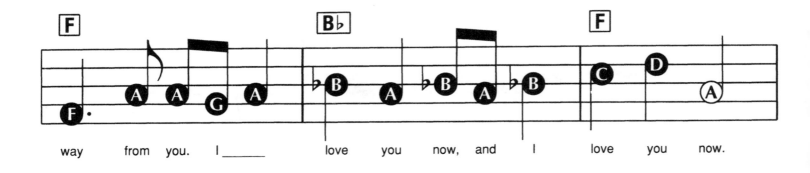

way from you. I _____ love you now, and I love you now.

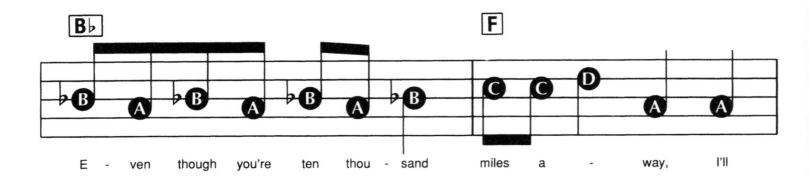

E - ven though you're ten thou - sand miles a - way, I'll

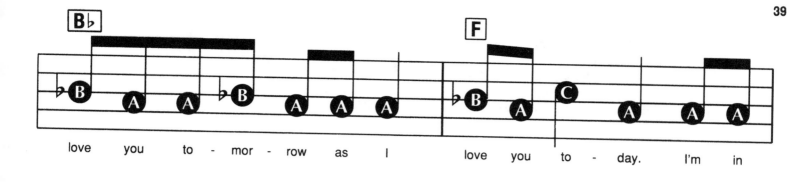

love you to - mor - row as I love you to - day. I'm in

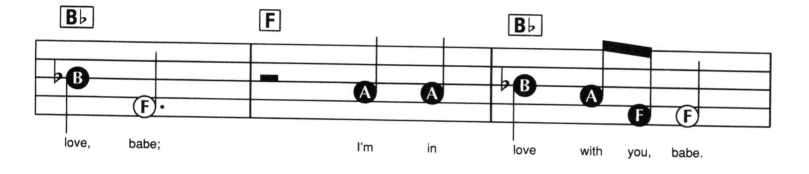

love, babe; I'm in love with you, babe.

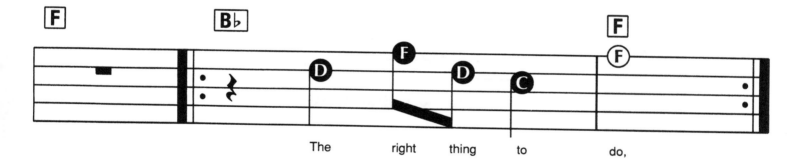

The right thing to do,

Additional Lyrics

2. Oh, I know you've had some bad luck with ladies before;
They drove you or you drove them crazy.
But more important is I know you're the one, and I'm sure;
Lovin' you's the right thing to do; lovin' you's the right thing.

3. You hold me in your hands like a bunch of flowers;
Set me movin' to your sweetest song.
And I know what I think I've known all along;
Lovin' you's the right thing to do; lovin' you's the right thing.
(To Coda:)

That's The Way I've Always Heard It Should Be

Registration 9
Rhythm: Slow Rock or 12 Beat

Words and Music by Carly Simon
and Jacob Brackman

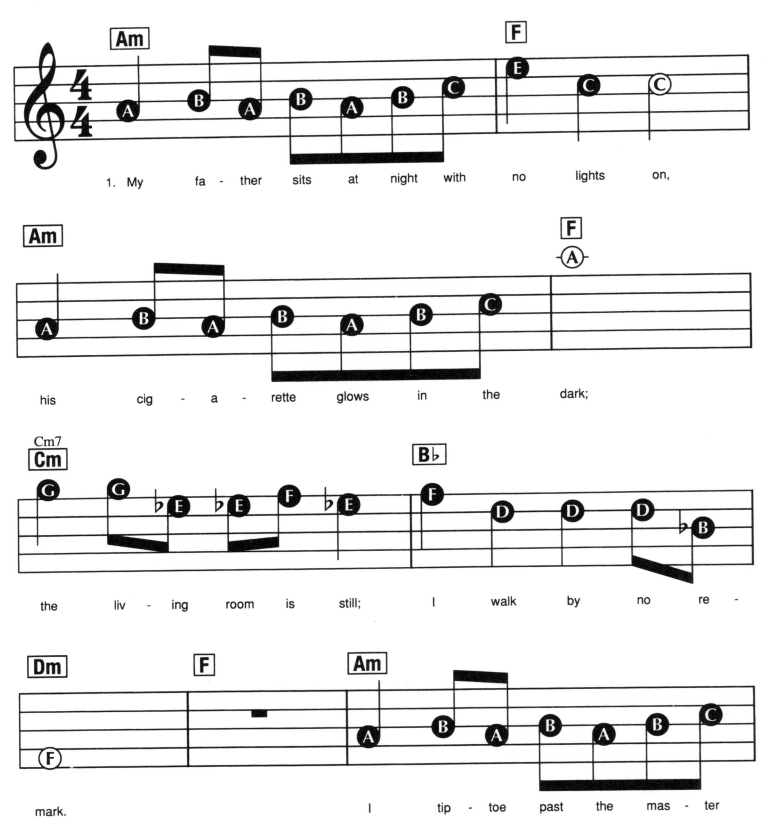

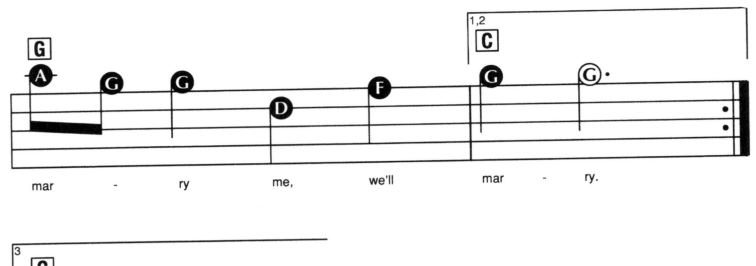

mar - ry me, we'll mar - ry.

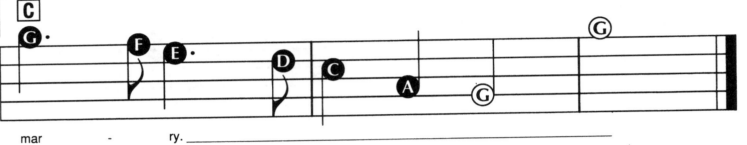

mar - ry.

Additional Lyrics

2. My friends from college, they're all married now; they have their houses and their lawns.
   They have their silent noons, tearful nights, angry dawns.
   Their children hate them for the things they're not; they hate themselves for what they are;
   And yet they drink, they laugh, close the wounds, hide the scar.

   (To Chorus:)

3. You say that we can keep our love alive. Babe, all I know is what I see.
   The couples cling and claw and drown in love's debris.
   You say we'll soar like two birds thru the clouds, but soon you'll cage me on your shelf.
   I'll never learn to be just me first, by myself.

   (To Chorus:)

You Belong to Me

Registration 5
Rhythm: Disco or 16 Beat

Words and Music by Carly Simon
and Michael McDonald

44

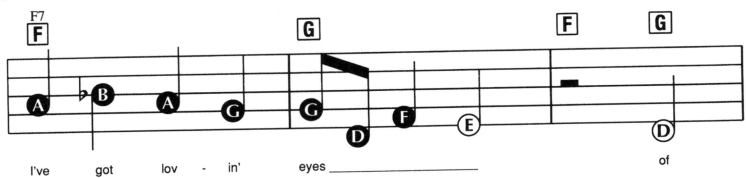

I've got lov - in' eyes _____ of

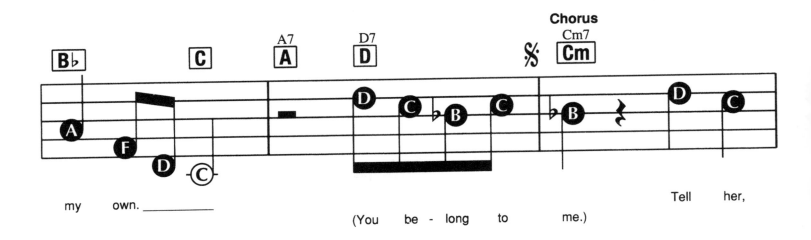

my own. _____ (You be - long to me.) Tell her,

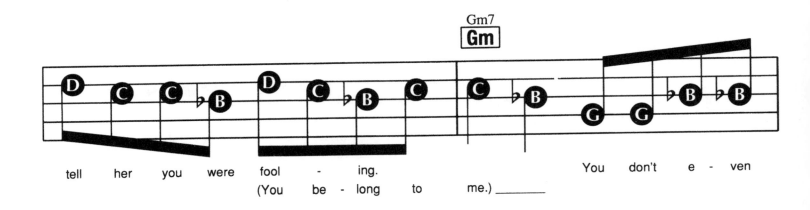

tell her you were fool - ing. You don't e - ven
(You be - long to me.) _____

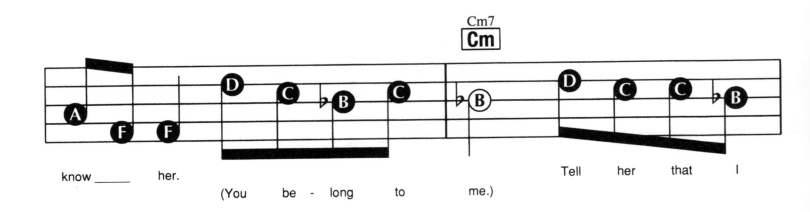

know _____ her. Tell her that I
(You be - long to me.)

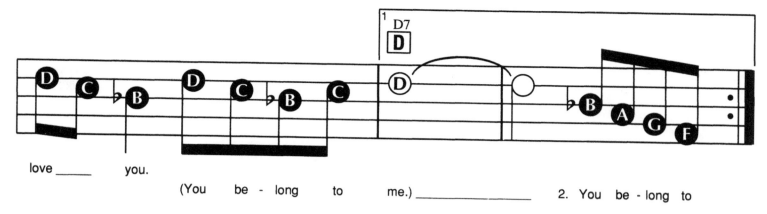

love _____ you.

(You be - long to me.) _____ 2. You be - long to

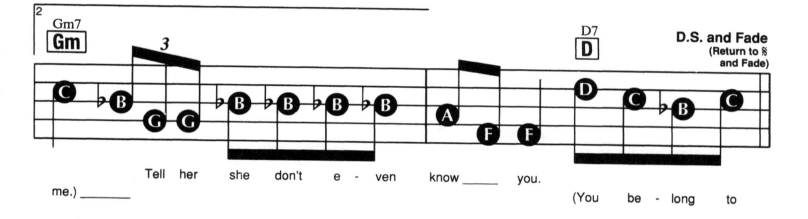

me.) _____

Tell her she don't e - ven know _____ you.

(You be - long to

Additional Lyrics

2. You belong to me. Can it be that you're not sure?
   You belong to me. Thought we'd closed the book, locked the door.
   You don't have to prove to me that you're beautiful to strangers.
   Well, I've got loving eyes of my own, and I can tell . . .

Chorus 2:

(You belong to me.) Tell her that I love you.
(You belong to me.) You belong, you belong, you belong to me.
(You belong to me.) Tell her you were fooling.
(You belong to me.) Tell her she don't even know you.

You're So Vain

Registration 2
Rhythm: Rock or 8 Beat

Words and Music by
Carly Simon

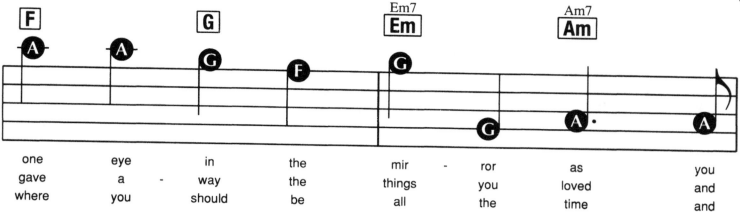

one eye in the mir - ror as you
gave a - way the things you as loved you
where you should be all the time and

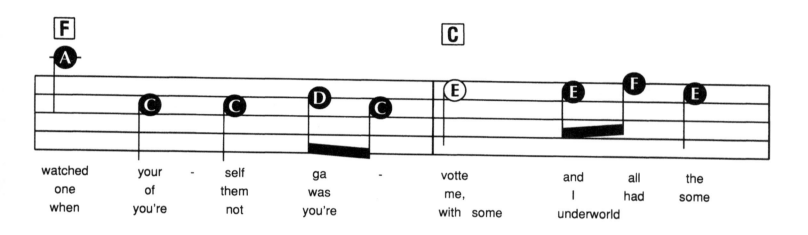

watched your - self ga - votte and all the
one of them was me, I had some
when you're not you're with some underworld

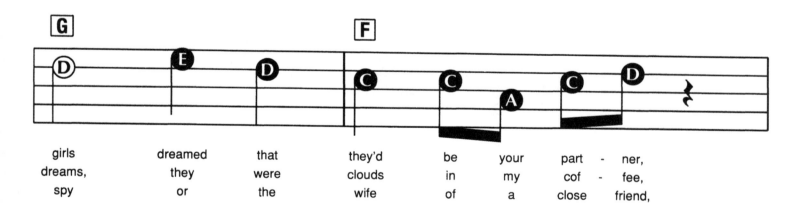

girls dreamed that they'd be your part - ner,
dreams, they were clouds in my cof - fee,
spy or the wife of a close friend,

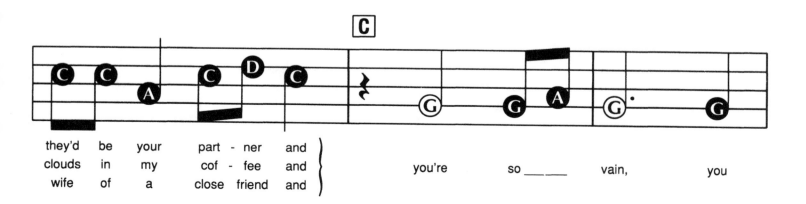

they'd be your part - ner and
clouds in my cof - fee and
wife of a close friend and

you're so _____ vain, you

48

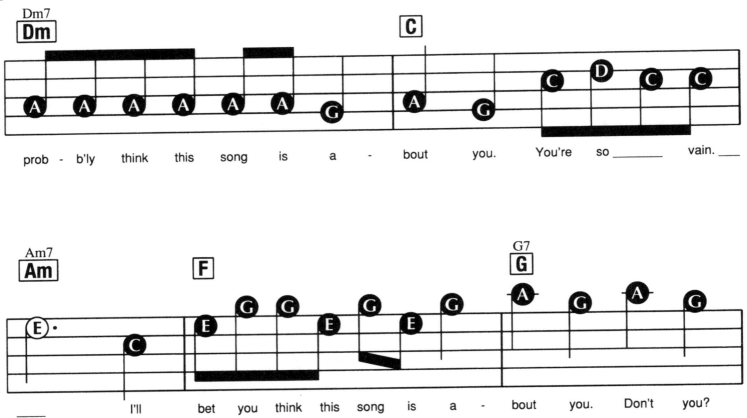

prob - b'ly think this song is a - bout you. You're so _____ vain. ___

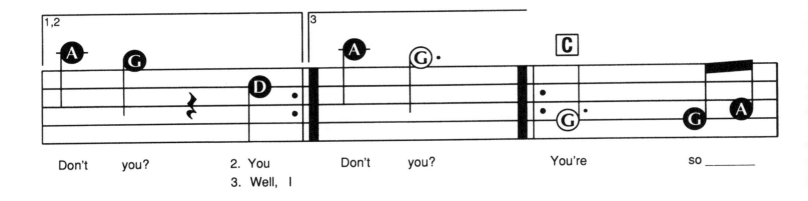

___ I'll bet you think this song is a - bout you. Don't you?

1,2   3

Don't you?   2. You   Don't you?   You're   so _____
             3. Well, I

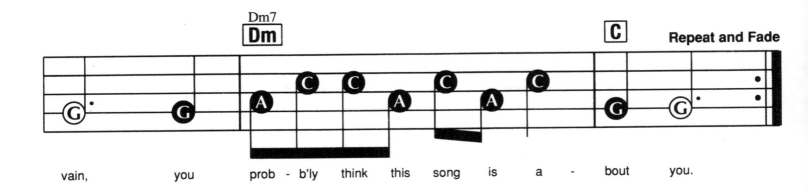

Repeat and Fade

vain,   you   prob - b'ly think this song is a - bout you.